JOHN THOMPSON'S
EASIEST PIANO COURSE
FIRST MUSICALS

Teachers and Parents. This collection of showtunes, arranged in the John Thompson tradition, is intended as supplementary material for advancing young pianists in the Easiest Piano Course or other similar methods. Listed in the suggested order of study, most students can begin playing the simpler arrangements after Part 1, and the difficulty progresses through to Parts 3 and 4. The pieces may also be used for sight-reading practice by more advanced students.

Arranged by Christopher Hussey

ISBN 978-1-70513-175-6

WILLIS MUSIC

EXCLUSIVELY DISTRIBUTED BY

HAL•LEONARD®

Visit Hal Leonard Online at
www.halleonard.com

Contact us:
Hal Leonard
7777 West Bluemound Road
Milwaukee, WI 53213
Email: info@halleonard.com

In Europe, contact:
Hal Leonard Europe Limited
42 Wigmore Street
Marylebone, London, W1U 2RN
Email: info@halleonardeurope.com

In Australia, contact:
Hal Leonard Australia Pty. Ltd.
4 Lentara Court
Cheltenham, Victoria, 3192 Australia
Email: info@halleonard.com.au

The Music of the Night
from THE PHANTOM OF THE OPERA

Music by Andrew Lloyd Webber
Lyrics by Charles Hart
Additional Lyrics by Richard Stilgoe

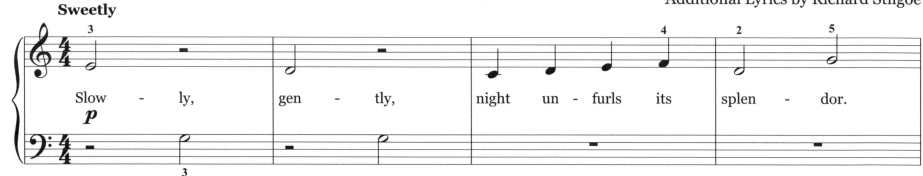

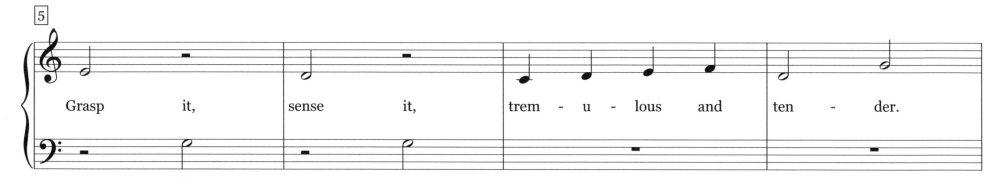

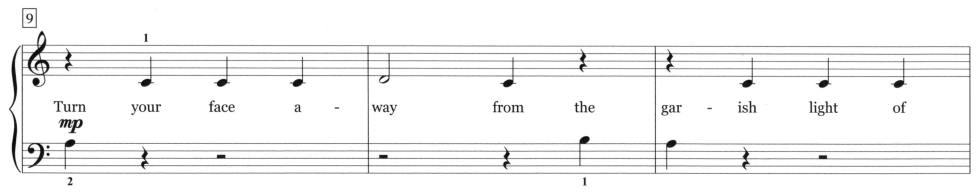

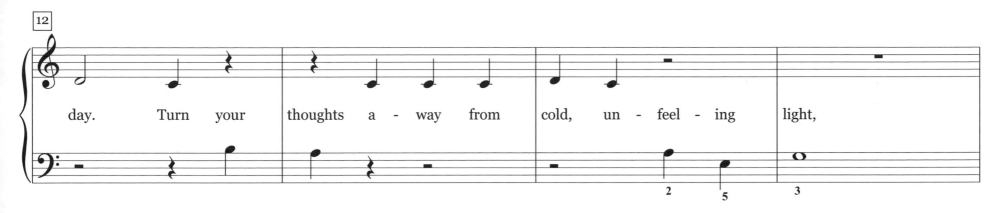

day. Turn your thoughts a — way from cold, un — feel — ing light,

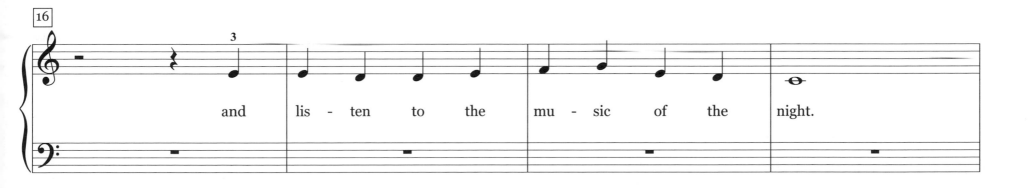

and lis — ten to the mu — sic of the night.

For Good

from the Broadway Musical WICKED

Music and Lyrics by
Stephen Schwartz

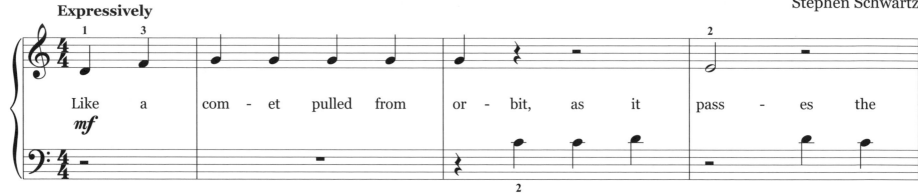

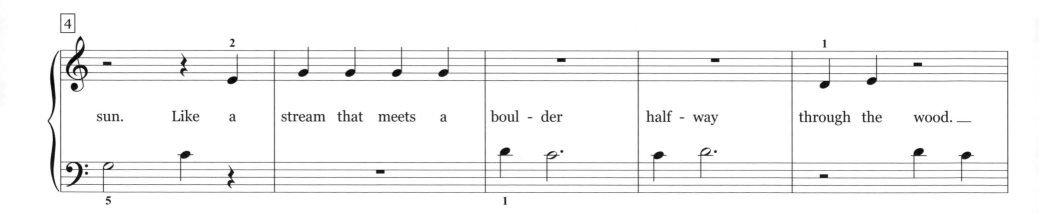

5

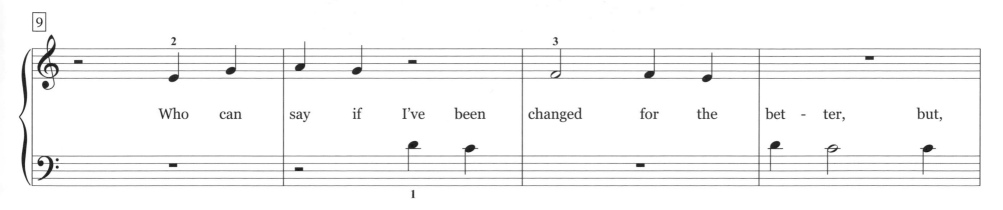

Who can say if I've been changed for the bet - ter, but,

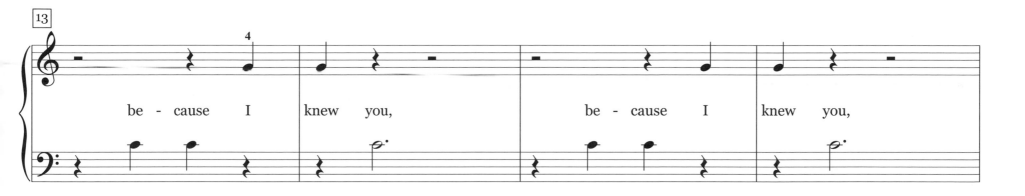

be - cause I knew you, be - cause I knew you,

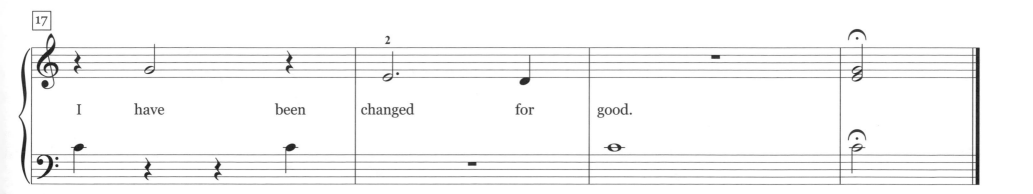

I have been changed for good.

Beauty and the Beast

from BEAUTY AND THE BEAST: THE BROADWAY MUSICAL

Music by Alan Menken
Lyrics by Howard Ashman

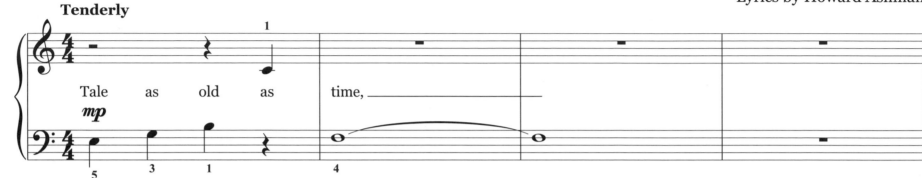

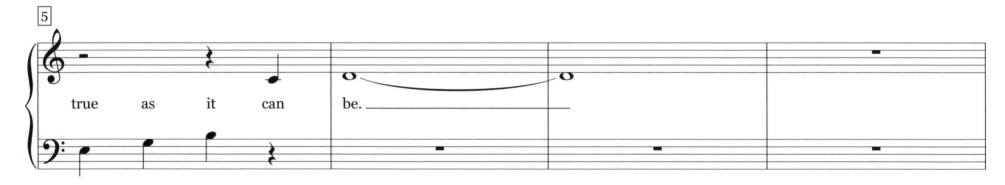

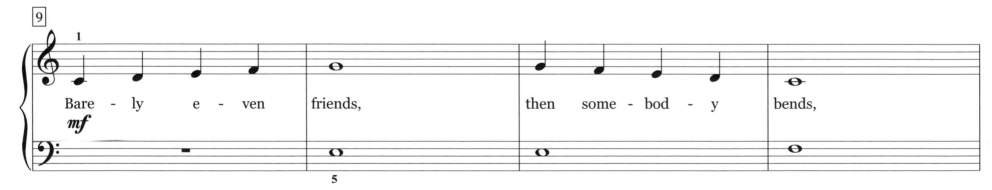

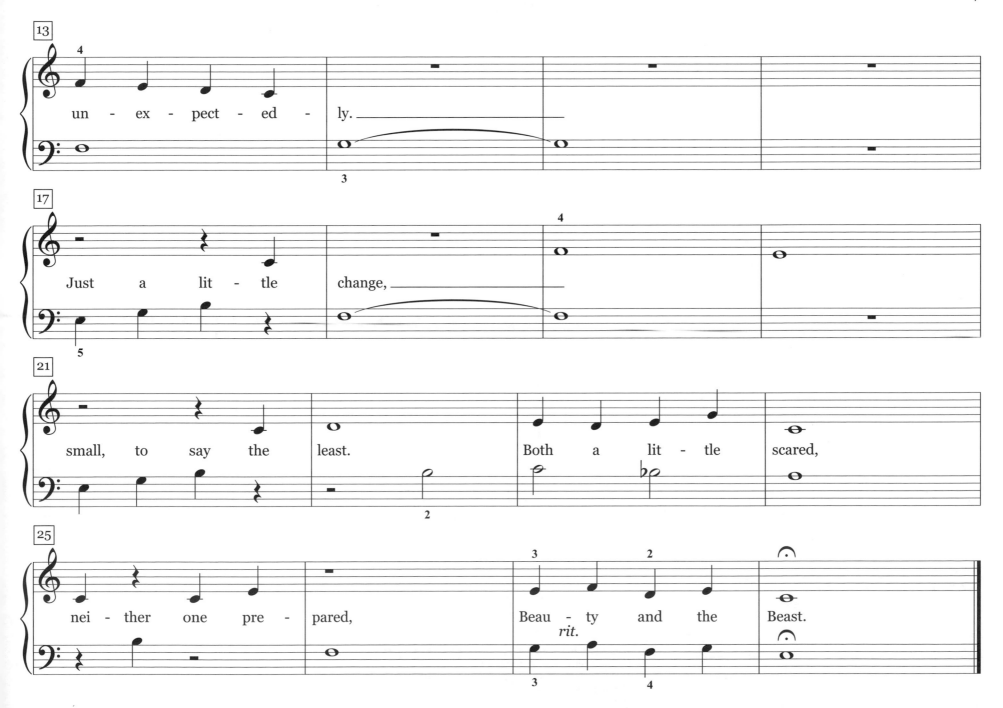

8

Memory
from CATS

Music by Andrew Lloyd Webber
Text by Trevor Nunn after T.S. Eliot

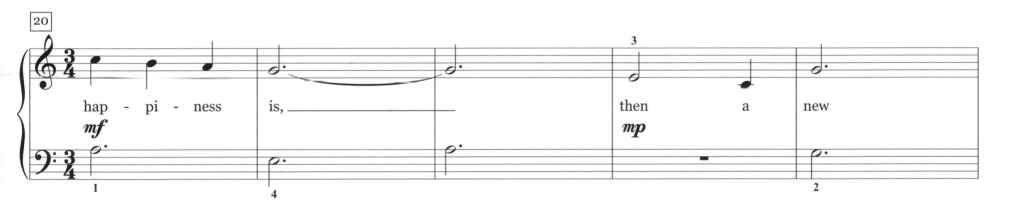

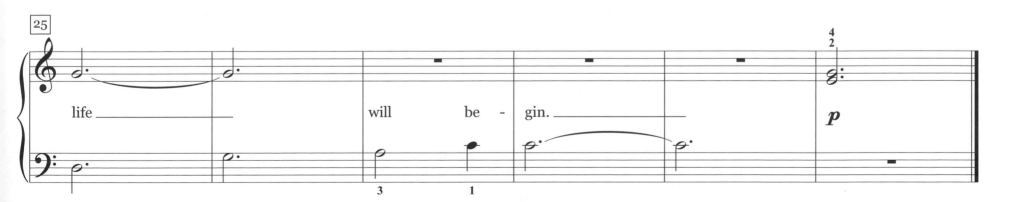

On My Own

from LES MISÉRABLES

Music by Claude-Michel Schönberg
Lyrics by Alain Boublil, Jean-Marc Natel,
Herbert Kretzmer, John Caird and Trevor Nunn

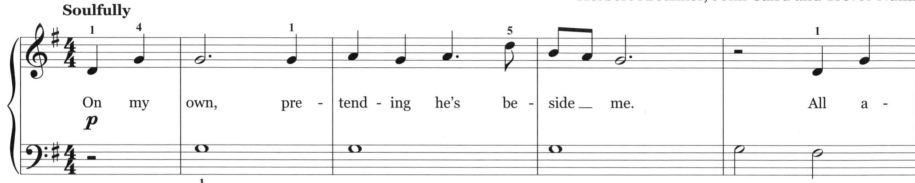

Chim Chim Cher-ee

from MARY POPPINS

Words and Music by Richard M. Sherman
and Robert B. Sherman

Chim, chim - i - ney, chim, chim - i - ney, chim, chim, cher - oo, good

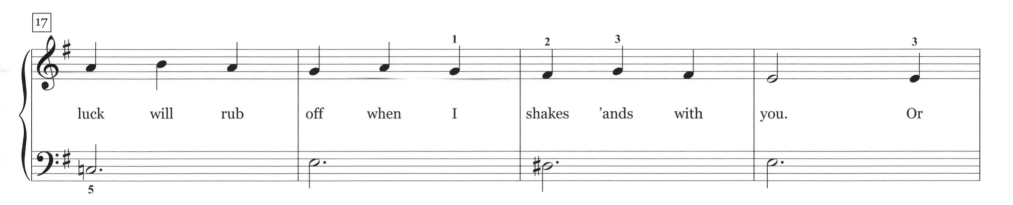

luck will rub off when I shakes 'ands with you. Or

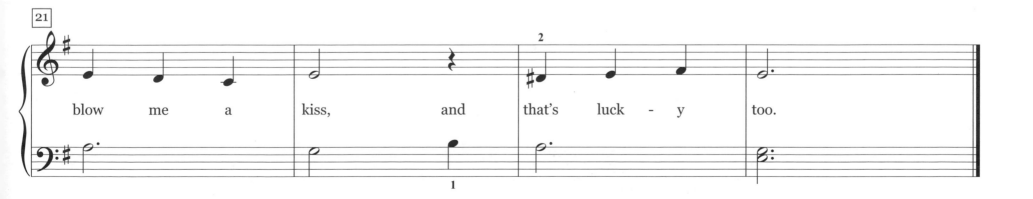

blow me a kiss, and that's luck - y too.

14

School of Rock
from SCHOOL OF ROCK

Words and Music by Mike White
and Samuel Buonaugurio

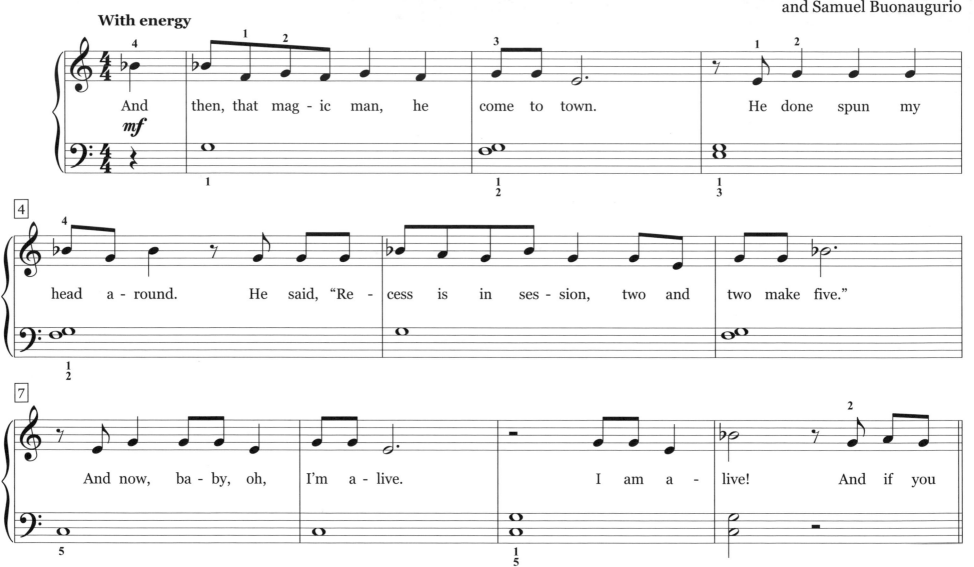

You Will Be Found

from DEAR EVAN HANSEN

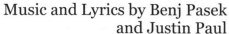

Music and Lyrics by Benj Pasek
and Justin Paul

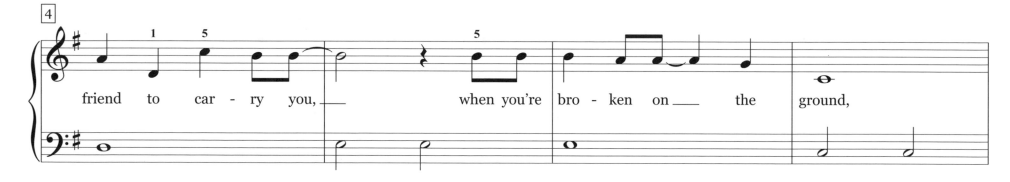

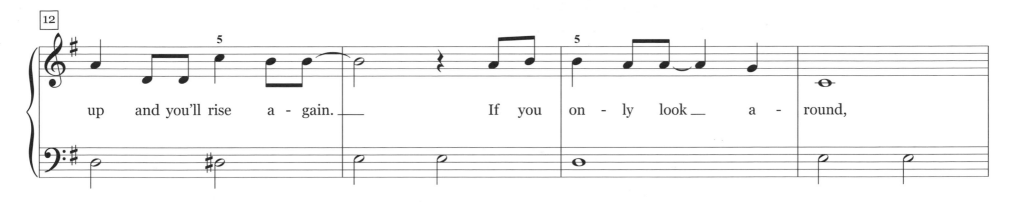

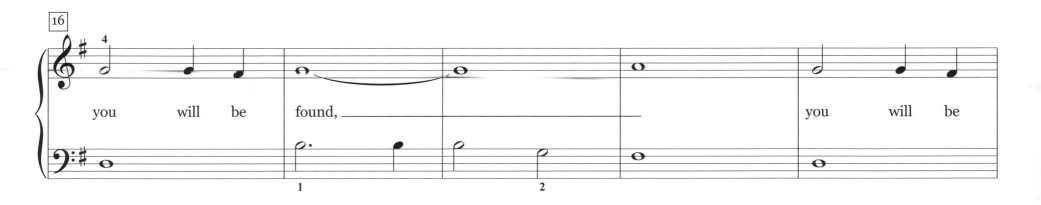

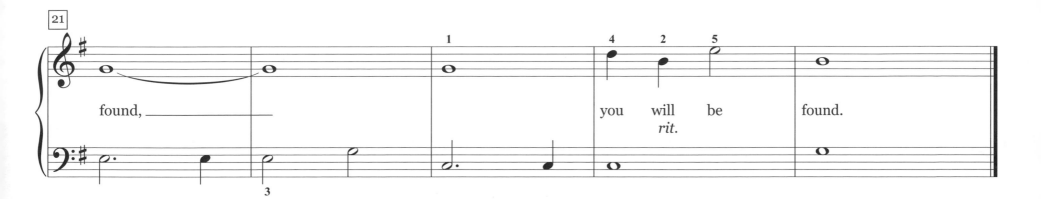

Hakuna Matata

Disney Presents THE LION KING: THE BROADWAY MUSICAL

Music by Elton John
Lyrics by Tim Rice

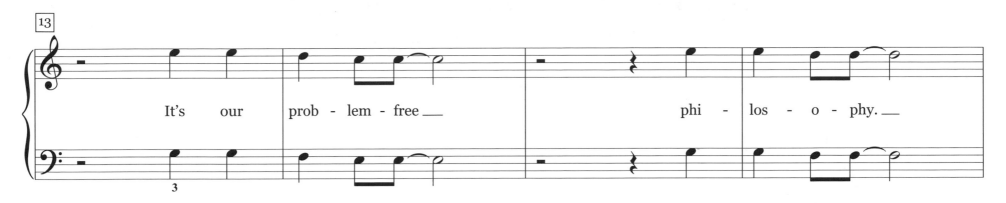

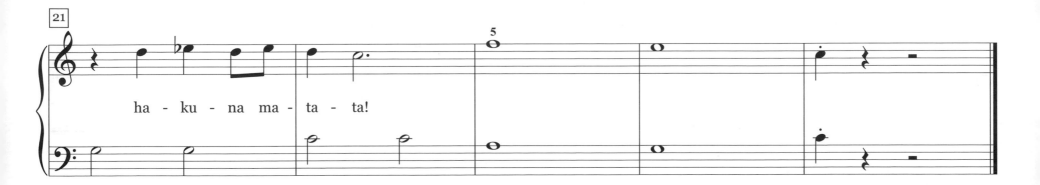

We're All in This Together

from HIGH SCHOOL MUSICAL

Words and Music by Matthew Gerrard
and Robbie Nevil

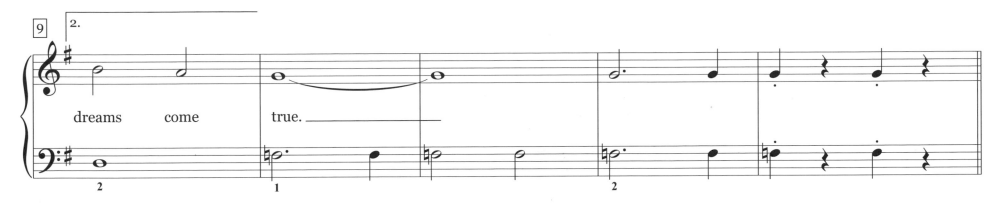

dreams come true. _____

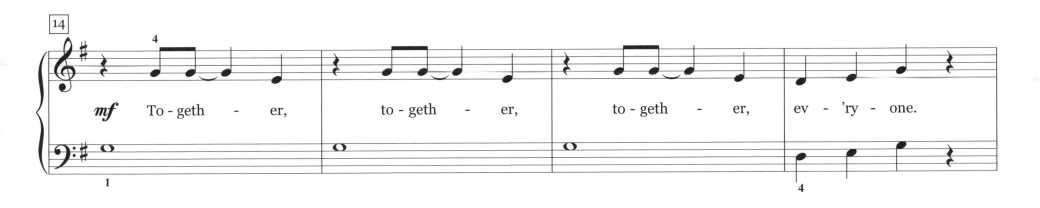

mf To - geth - er, to - geth - er, to - geth - er, ev - 'ry - one.

To - geth - er, to - geth - er, come on, ___ let's have some fun.

City of Stars

from LA LA LAND

Music by Justin Hurwitz
Lyrics by Benj Pasek & Justin Paul

now, our dreams, they've fi - n'lly come true.

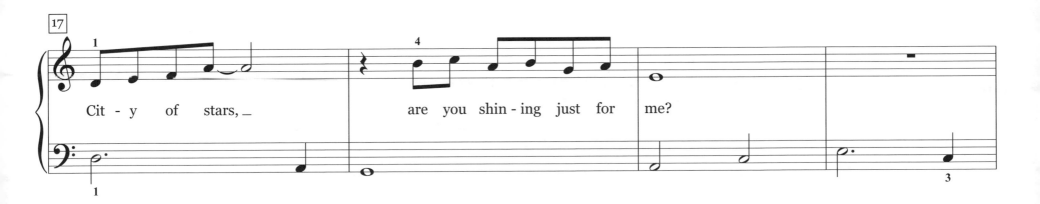

Cit - y of stars, __ are you shin - ing just for me?

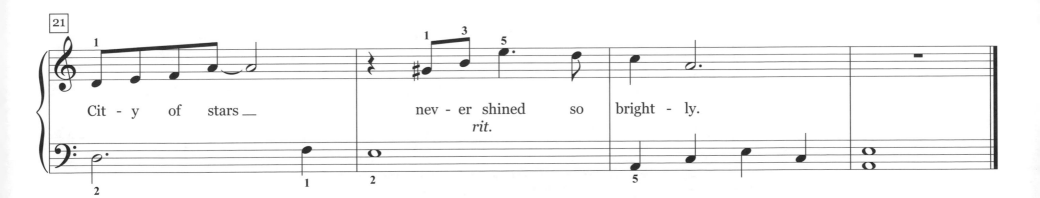

Cit - y of stars __ nev - er shined so bright - ly.

rit.

Naughty

from MATILDA THE MUSICAL

Words and Music by
Tim Minchin

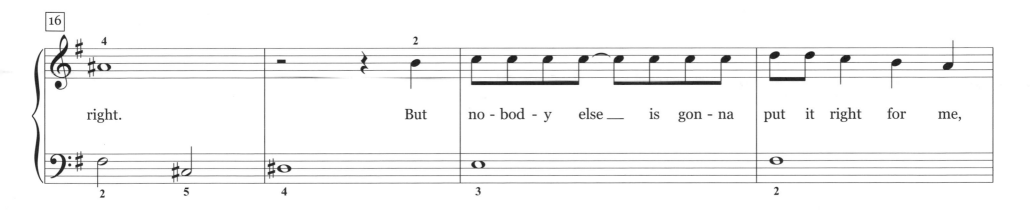
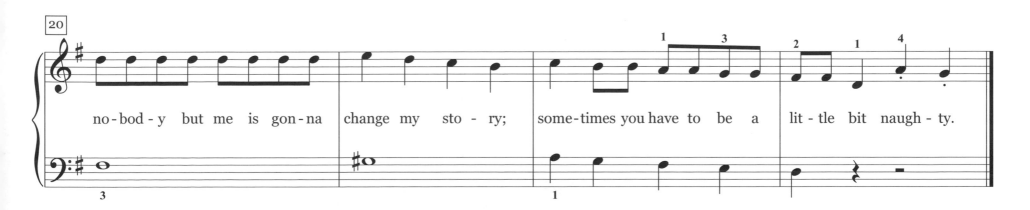

This Is Me
from THE GREATEST SHOWMAN

Words and Music by Benj Pasek
and Justin Paul

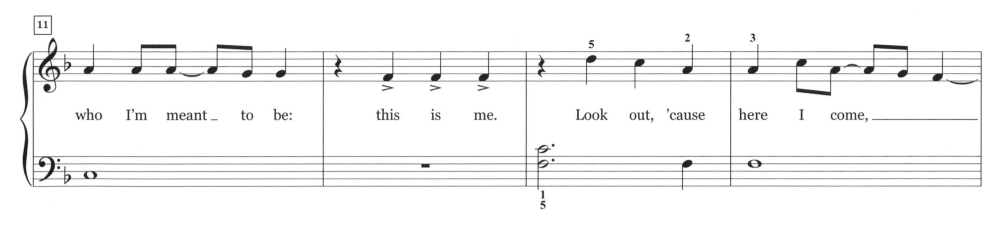

who I'm meant _ to be: this is me. Look out, 'cause here I come, _____

_____ and I'm march-ing on to the beat I drum. _____

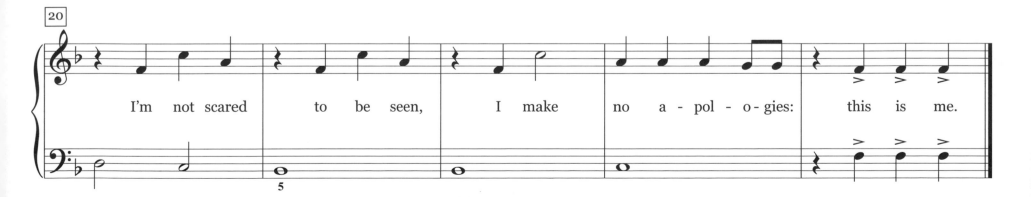

I'm not scared to be seen, I make no a-pol-o-gies: this is me.

Speechless

from ALADDIN

Music by Alan Menken
Lyrics by Benj Pasek and Justin Paul

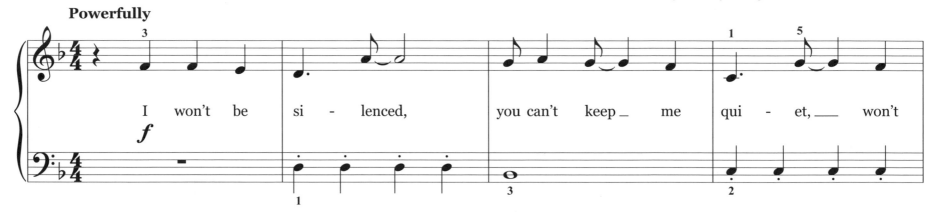

I won't be si - lenced, you can't keep me qui - et, won't

trem - ble when you try it. All I know is I won't go speech - less.

'Cause — I'll breathe — when they try to suf - fo - cate me. — Don't you

un - der - es - ti - mate me, 'cause I know — that I won't — go speech-less. All I know —

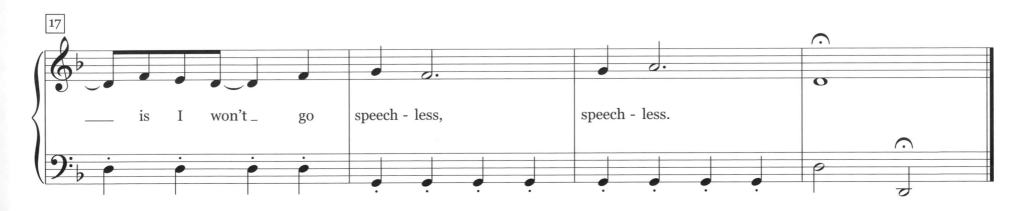

— is I won't — go speech - less, speech - less.

Trip a Little Light Fantastic

from MARY POPPINS RETURNS

Music by Marc Shaiman
Lyrics by Scott Wittman and Marc Shaiman

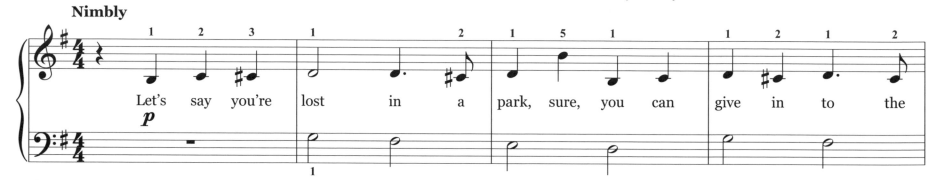

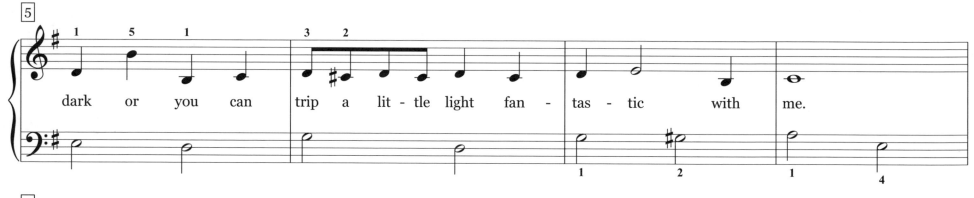

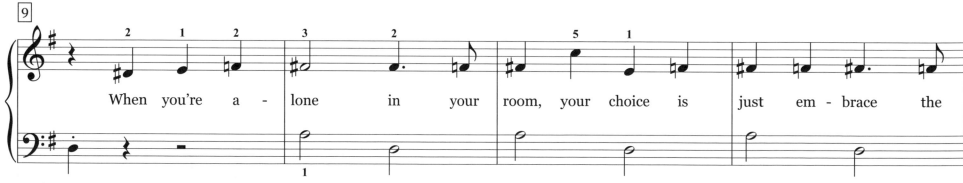

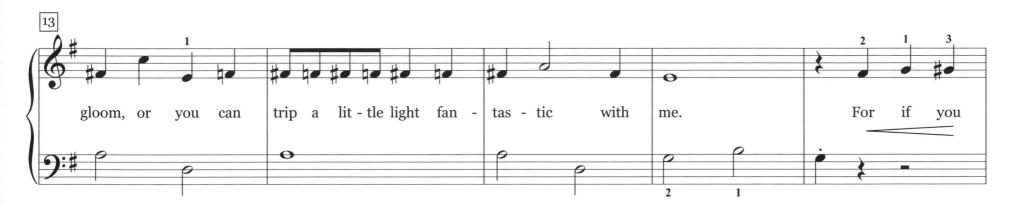

gloom, or you can trip a lit - tle light fan - tas - tic with me. For if you

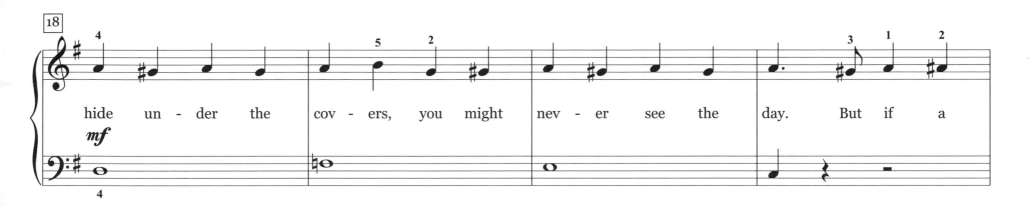

hide un - der the cov - ers, you might nev - er see the day. But if a

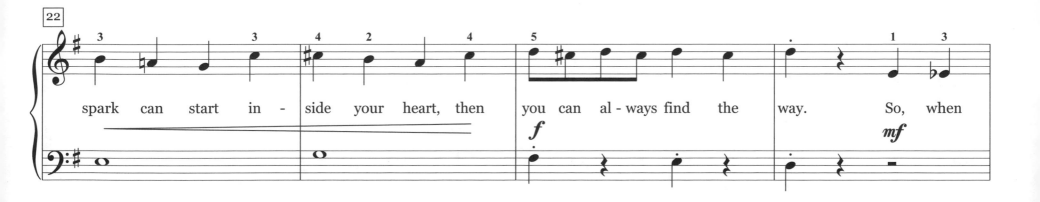

spark can start in - side your heart, then you can al - ways find the way. So, when

32